the gift of gopal

Adapted by Sita Gilbakian
Illustrated by Padmavati Devi Dasi

MANDALA
publishing group

From Ancient India come the mystical and enchanting stories of Gopal, the cowherder.

While living the life of a simple village boy, Gopal is actually God himself playing human. His adventures in the forests of Vrindavan bring both joy and amazement to those who hear them.

Endowed with limitless powers and riches, Gopal shows time and time again his greatest strength is his love and affection for his cows, friends and family.

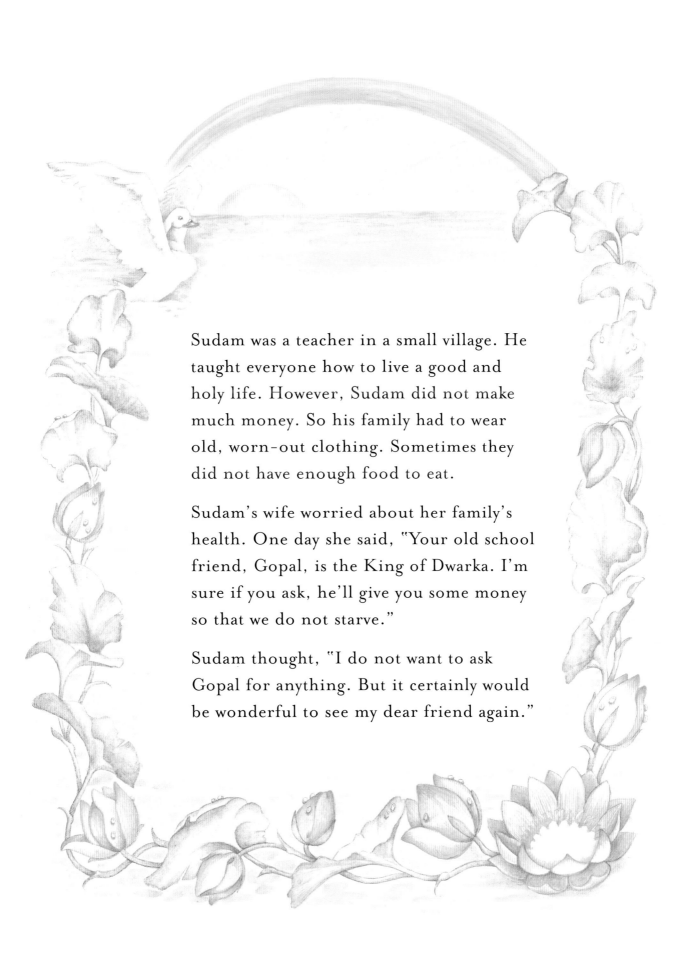

Sudam was a teacher in a small village. He taught everyone how to live a good and holy life. However, Sudam did not make much money. So his family had to wear old, worn-out clothing. Sometimes they did not have enough food to eat.

Sudam's wife worried about her family's health. One day she said, "Your old school friend, Gopal, is the King of Dwarka. I'm sure if you ask, he'll give you some money so that we do not starve."

Sudam thought, "I do not want to ask Gopal for anything. But it certainly would be wonderful to see my dear friend again."

So Sudam agreed to his wife's plan. But he said, "I cannot go empty-handed. Is there a gift I could bring Gopal?" His wife looked in the cupboard. "We have nothing in our house," She said. "Our neighbors are generous," Sudam suggested. "Perhaps they will give something."

Sudam's wife begged four palmfuls of broken rice from their poor neighbors. She tied the rice in a small cloth and gave it to Sudam. "I know these are only a few grains of rice," she said, "but it will have to do."

Sudam then set off for the royal city of Dwarka with this humble gift.

Sudam walked through the forest on the way to Dwarka. It reminded him of one special time when their teacher had sent Gopal and Sudam to collect firewood.

The day had been warm and sunny with a gentle wind. As the boys gathered their bundles of firewood, they played in the long forest grasses. They swam in the cool waters of an inviting pool.

Swinging from tree branches, they imitated the forest monkeys. The gusty wind was perfect for floating dry leaves. The boys threw them into the air and the wind blew the leaves in all directions.

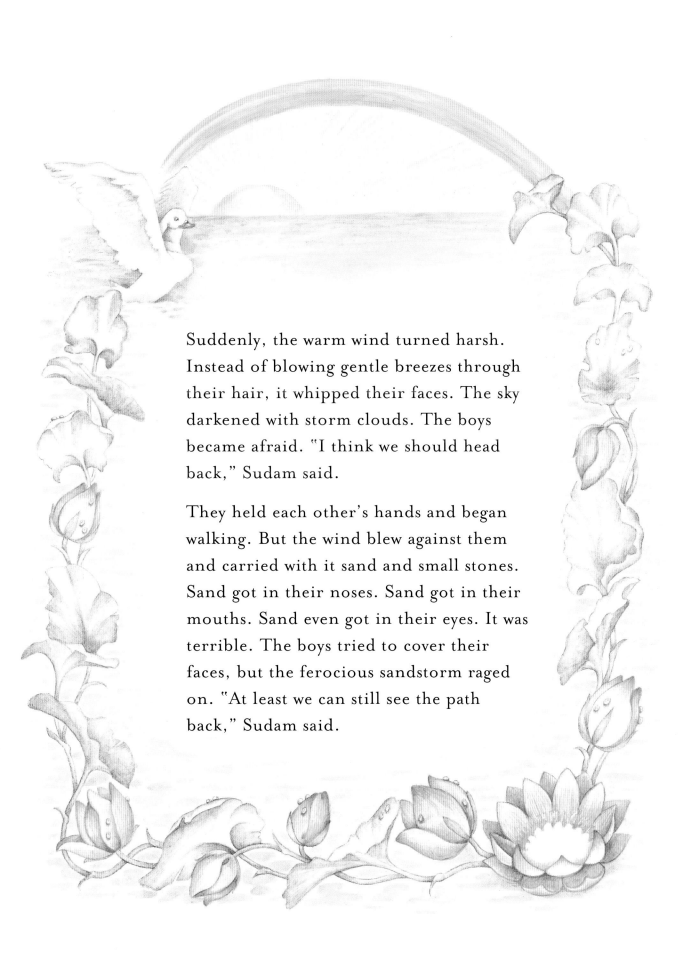

Suddenly, the warm wind turned harsh.
Instead of blowing gentle breezes through
their hair, it whipped their faces. The sky
darkened with storm clouds. The boys
became afraid. "I think we should head
back," Sudam said.

They held each other's hands and began
walking. But the wind blew against them
and carried with it sand and small stones.
Sand got in their noses. Sand got in their
mouths. Sand even got in their eyes. It was
terrible. The boys tried to cover their
faces, but the ferocious sandstorm raged
on. "At least we can still see the path
back," Sudam said.

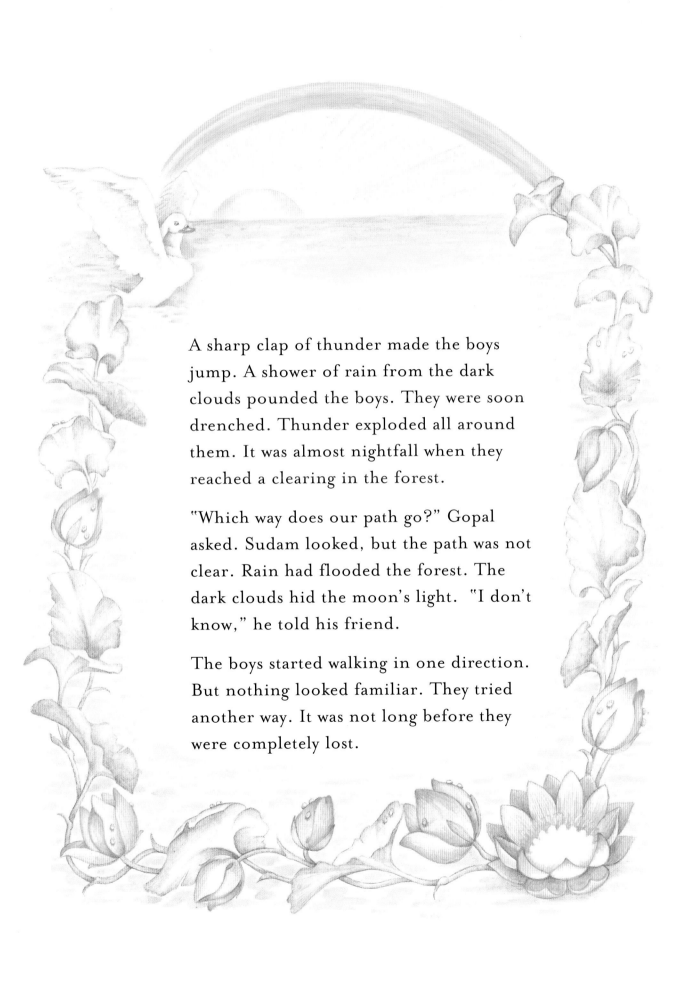

A sharp clap of thunder made the boys jump. A shower of rain from the dark clouds pounded the boys. They were soon drenched. Thunder exploded all around them. It was almost nightfall when they reached a clearing in the forest.

"Which way does our path go?" Gopal asked. Sudam looked, but the path was not clear. Rain had flooded the forest. The dark clouds hid the moon's light. "I don't know," he told his friend.

The boys started walking in one direction. But nothing looked familiar. They tried another way. It was not long before they were completely lost.

Back at the schoolhouse, their teacher was worried. Why hadn't the boys returned? He sent out a search party to look for them. They looked through the forest all night long, but they could not find Sudam and Gopal. At last, in the morning, they found the two friends. They were huddled together asleep under a bush.

Sandipani was so happy to find them alive. "You have suffered so much collecting this firewood. I bless you both. May you always have everything you need."

Just remembering all this made Sudam feel happy. And so his journey to Dwarka quickly passed.

A boatman ferried Sudam to the entrance of the seaside city of Dwarka. Sudam could not believe his eyes. The magnificent city was unlike anything he could have imagined. He walked up a long marble stairway to the city gates. Everyone greeted him as a welcome guest. Sudam strolled through the beautiful gardens to the town center. Golden domes of hundreds of beautiful palaces glittered in the bright sunlight. Rolling parks with clear lakes graced every corner of the city. It was all so different from his poor village.

"I hope that my friend Gopal remembers me," Sudam thought.

Sudam felt as if he were in another world. The fruits and flowers on the trees lining Dwarka's wide roads smelled intoxicatingly sweet. Each palace he passed was more dazzling than the last. When he came to the most splendid palace of all he asked, "Who lives here?" "The King and Queen of Dwarka," the palace doorman answered.

Sudam looked down at his bare feet, dirty from walking so far. He touched the holes in his clothes. "I do not think that I should enter such a grand palace." Just then Gopal came out. He embraced Sudam with great affection.

Gopal took Sudam's hand. "You must be tired from such a long journey. Come sit on my bed." Sudam did not want to get Gopal's richly decorated bed dirty. But Gopal insisted and even washed Sudam's dusty feet! Gopal said, "You must be very hot. Let me rub some cooling sandalwood paste on your body."

Queen Rukmini brought sweets, fruits and drinks for Sudam. Then she fanned Sudam with a yak-tail fan. Sudam did not feel he should be receiving so much attention from the King and Queen. He felt that he should be fanning and serving Gopal and his beautiful Queen Rukmini.

Gopal sat Sudam beside him on his kingly throne. He asked, "Do you remember our teacher's wife?" Sudam laughed. "She made sweets for us." "Oh yes," Gopal said. "I remember eating far too much of her wonderful cooking."

Gopal fingered his ornate silk robe. "Even then I liked rich things." Sudam looked at his own ragged clothes. He felt so different from his schoolmate.

"You never desired to be very wealthy," Gopal said. Then he added, "But if you ever were offered riches, you should take them. Use them to help the poor."

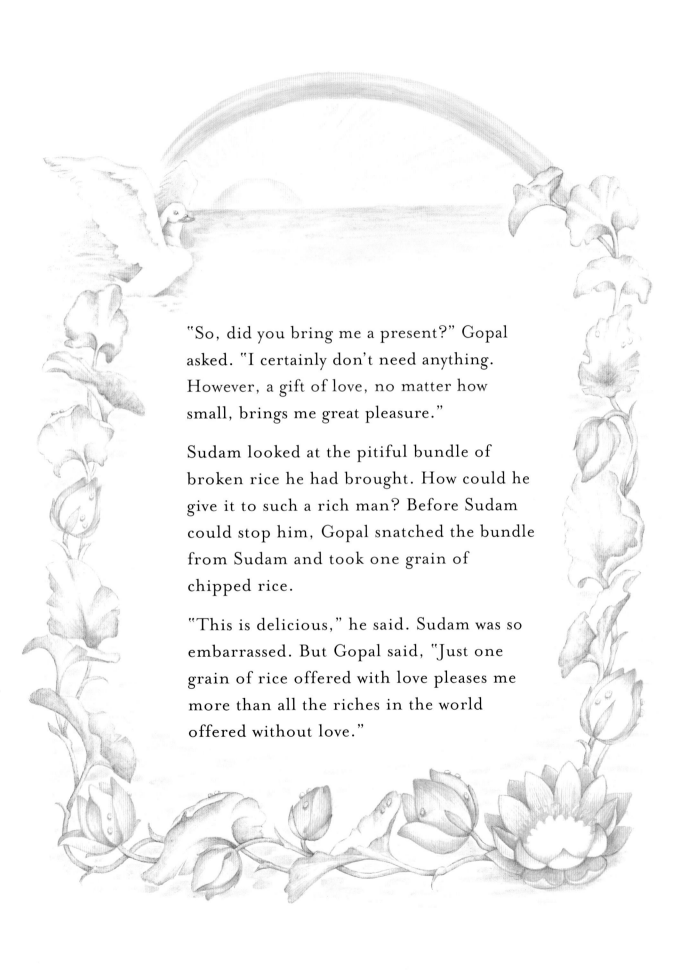

"So, did you bring me a present?" Gopal asked. "I certainly don't need anything. However, a gift of love, no matter how small, brings me great pleasure."

Sudam looked at the pitiful bundle of broken rice he had brought. How could he give it to such a rich man? Before Sudam could stop him, Gopal snatched the bundle from Sudam and took one grain of chipped rice.

"This is delicious," he said. Sudam was so embarrassed. But Gopal said, "Just one grain of rice offered with love pleases me more than all the riches in the world offered without love."

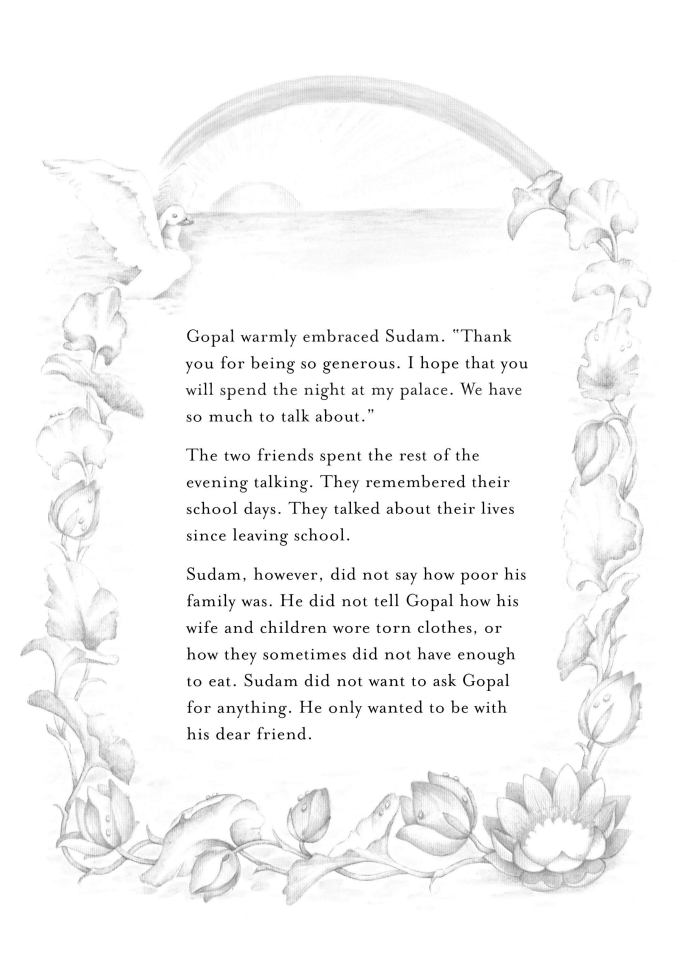

Gopal warmly embraced Sudam. "Thank you for being so generous. I hope that you will spend the night at my palace. We have so much to talk about."

The two friends spent the rest of the evening talking. They remembered their school days. They talked about their lives since leaving school.

Sudam, however, did not say how poor his family was. He did not tell Gopal how his wife and children wore torn clothes, or how they sometimes did not have enough to eat. Sudam did not want to ask Gopal for anything. He only wanted to be with his dear friend.

Sudam left Dwarka the next morning.
As he walked home through the forest he
thought, "How fortunate I am. Even
though Gopal is such a great king, he
embraced a poor teacher like me. He
even massaged my legs. My wife will not
believe this!"

When Sudam thought of his wife, he
remembered that he had not asked Gopal
for any help. "Oh well," he thought.
"I think Gopal did not give me any riches
because he knew that if I became wealthy
I would soon forget him. I'm sure my wife
will understand. We can get by with what
we have."

Sudam rounded the final bend in the road. "Have I come to the wrong village?" he wondered. Where his run-down cottage used to be, there stood a majestic marble palace decorated with ivory and gold. Gardens and lakes filled with lotus flowers surrounded it. Sudam hardly recognized his wife. She was not wearing old rags. She did not look weak from hunger. She looked like a queen.

"These are gifts from my dear friend Gopal," Sudam said. "I just gave him a broken grain of rice, and he has given us all this. I did not even tell him that we needed anything."

A sumptuous meal was prepared for them in their beautiful dining room. Sudam's daughter and son greeted him there. He hugged them tightly and kissed their heads. Sudam asked them, "Did I ever tell you the story about the little sparrow who built her nest right by the ocean's shore?" "Please tell us," the children said.

Sudam began, "A mother sparrow was about to lay some eggs. She worked hard to build a strong and safe nest for her children. She chose to build it on the sandy shore of the ocean. She laid her eggs in the nest and waited for them to hatch."

The ocean waves lapping against the sand sounded so pleasant. It was a peaceful place to make a nest. Then one day the winds blew stronger. Clouds covered the sun. A storm churned the ocean. The once gentle waves rose high, their foamy heads menacing the shore. The mother sparrow grew afraid, but she could not move her nest without hurting her eggs. She flew above the ocean's waves and cried, "Oh please Great Ocean, do not wash up on the shore near my nest. Please do not take my children from me."

The vast ocean did not listen to the tiny sparrow's pleas. Its waves continued bashing against the sandy shore, coming closer and closer to her nest. The sparrow watched as the ocean water washed all around her nest. There was nothing she could do. Then, with one mighty swoop, the ocean's waves scooped up the sparrow's nest.

The mother sparrow let out an anguished cry. "My children! My poor children! Please give me back my children!" The ocean laughed at the sparrow. "Never. Your eggs are deep under my waters now." The tiny sparrow cried and cried. She felt all alone.

The tiny sparrow was not alone. Flying high in the sky above the ocean was a powerful eagle. The eagle saw what had happened and flew to the sparrow's side. The great eagle turned to the ocean. She shouted loudly, "I demand that you return the sparrow's nest immediately. If you do not, I, and all my brothers and sisters will suck your waters dry."

The ocean trembled at this threat. With a gentle wave, it returned the sparrow's nest to the sandy shore. The sparrow said, "Thank you so much. There is no way I can possibly repay your kindness."

"The eagle flew away to its home and the baby sparrows all safely hatched," Sudam told his children.

"That is a wonderful story," Sudam's wife said. "I think your friend, Gopal, is like that great eagle. "He has blessed us with greater riches than we could have imagined."

"All I ever wanted was to remain his friend," Sudam said. Then he added, "We should not become proud now. We are not the real owners of this wealth. It belongs to Gopal. We will use it to serve him. We will be a friend to everyone as he has been a friend to us."

This exciting new line of beautifully illustrated children's books presents a charming and endearing narrative of the pastimes of Gopal.

Miraculous Gopal

When the village of Vrindavan is inundated with torrential rains sent by the furious King of Heaven, Indra, Gopal displays his divinity by lifting Govardhan Hill and saving the cows and all of the inhabitants of Vrindavan. Indra is humbled and offers prayers to Gopal, accepting him as the Supreme Person.

$14.95 hardbound, 48 pages
Item 1211

Gopal the Infallible

This tale recounts the pastime of Brahma's attempt to trick Gopal by kidnapping all of the cowherd boys and their cows and hiding them. Brahma waits for Gopal's reation only to discover that the cowherd boys and cows are back where they belong. Gopal has tricked Brahma by expanding himself into replicates of his playmates. The cowherd children' parents are even fooled into treating Gopal's expansions (the Supreme Lord) as their own children. Brahma is the one who is bewildered in the end and surrenders to Gopal

$14.95 hardbound, 48 pages
Item 1212

Order now by calling 800 688 2218.
Have your Visa or Master Card ready.
Alternatively, send a check or money order to:
Mandala Publishing Group
103 Thomason Lane, Eugene, OR 97404

To our young readers
who are always eager
to hear the pastimes of
our friend Gopal.

Mandala Publishing Group
239C Joo Chait Road
Singapore 427496
65 342 3117 phone
65 342 3115 fax

103 Thomason Lane
Eugene, OR 97404 USA
541 688 2258 phone
541 461 3478 fax

1585-A Folsom Street
San Francisco, CA 94103 USA
415 626 1080 phone
415 626 1510 fax

mandala@mandala.org
www.mandala.org

Printed in Hong Kong through Palace Press International

ISBN 1-886069-19-0
Text © 1998 Mandala Publishing Group
Illustrations ® 1995 Attila Bakos and Agnes Vass

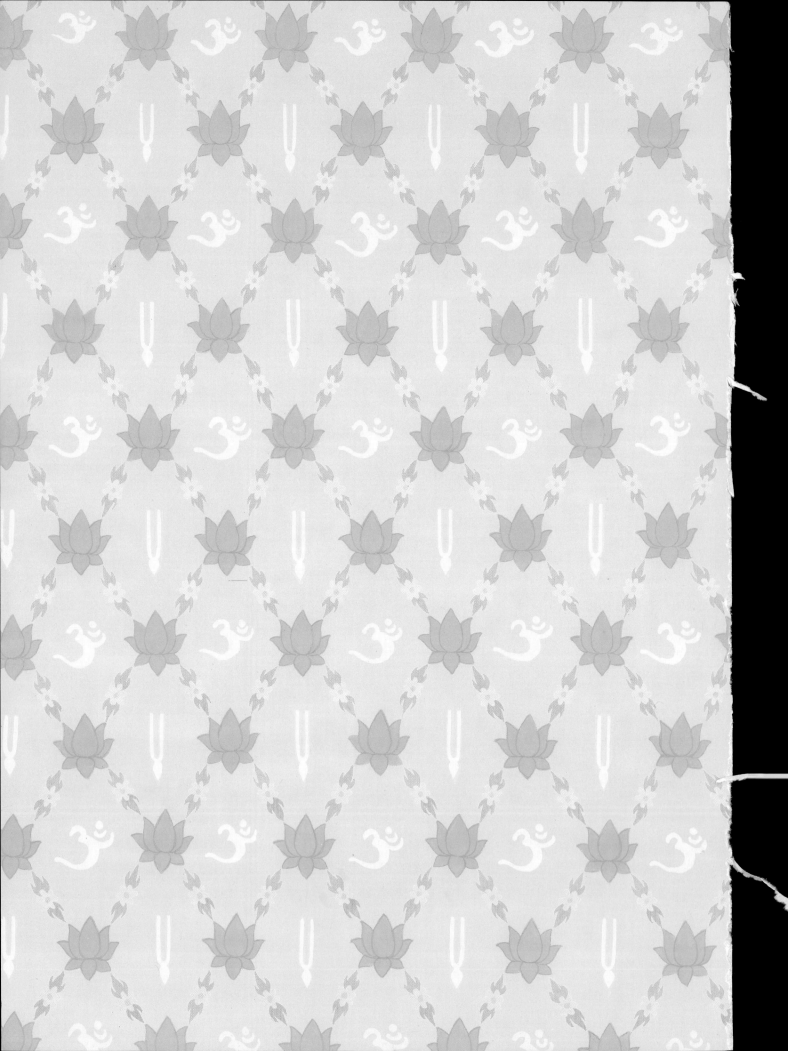